A Kid's Guide to Drawing the Countries of the World™

How to Draw
China's
Sights and Symbols

Melody S. Mis

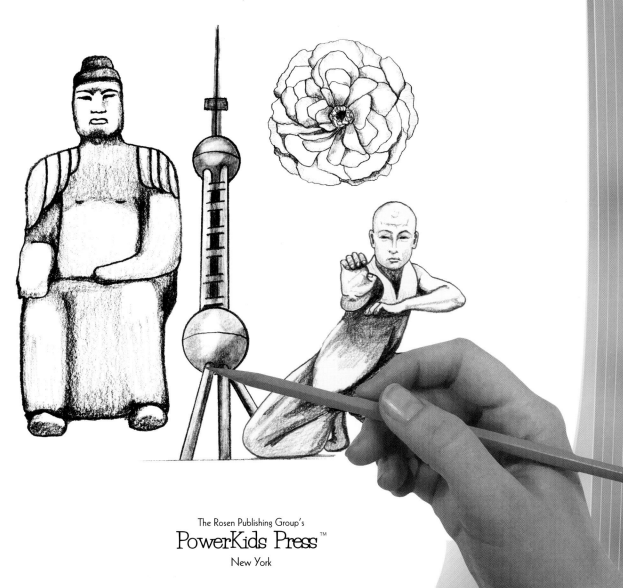

The Rosen Publishing Group's
PowerKids Press™
New York

To Connie and Paula for encouraging me to write

Published in 2004 by The Rosen Publishing Group, Inc.
29 East 21st Street, New York, NY 10010

First Edition

Editor: Jannell Khu
Book Design: Kim Sonsky
Layout Design: Michael de Guzman

Illustration Credits: Cover and inside by Emily Muschinske
Photo Credits: Cover and pp. 18, 34 © Keren Su/CORBIS; p. 5 © Joseph Sohm: ChromoSohm Inc./CORBIS; pp. 9, 22, 36 © Michael S. Yamashita/CORBIS; p. 10 © Charles E. Rotkin/CORBIS; p. 13 Ma Yuan, Chinese, active before 1189 to after 1225, Southern Song dynasty, *Watching the Deer by a Pine-Shaded Stream.* Ink and light color on silk, 24.8 x 26 cm. © The Cleveland Museum of Art, Gift of Mrs. A. Dean Perry, 1997.88; p. 20 © Peter Smithers/CORBIS; p. 24 (Skull) © Bettmann/CORBIS; p. 24 (Peking Man) © Dean Conger/CORBIS; p. 26 © Jack Fields/CORBIS; p. 28 © Wolfgang Kaehler/CORBIS; p. 30 © Dallas and John Heaton/CORBIS; p. 32 (sculpture) © Lowell Georgia/CORBIS; p. 32 (Museum) © Carl & Ann Purcell/CORBIS; p. 38 © Kevin Flemming/CORBIS; p. 40 (Goddess of Democracy) © Peter Turnley/CORBIS; p. 40 (Tiananmen Square) © Getty Images, Inc.; p. 42 © Bob Krist/CORBIS.

Mis, Melody S.
How to draw China's sights and symbols / Melody S. Mis.— 1st ed.
    p. cm. – (A kid's guide to drawing the countries of the world)
Summary: Presents step-by-step directions for drawing the national flag, Great Wall, a giant panda, and other sights and symbols of China.
Includes bibliographical references and index.
ISBN 0-8239-6664-X (library binding)
1. Drawing—Technique—Juvenile literature. 2. China—In art—Juvenile literature. [1. China—In art. 2. Drawing—Technique.] I. Title. II. Series.
NC655 .M573 2004
743'.93651—dc21
                                         2002153343

Manufactured in the United States of America

CONTENTS

Let's Draw China

China has one of the oldest civilizations in the world. China's written history dates from 4,000 years ago from the Shang dynasty. Dynasties ruled China until 1912. China is named for an ancient and important dynasty called Qin, which began in 221 B.C. Qin is pronounced "chin." Qin Shi Huang was the most famous leader of the Qin dynasty. He gave himself the title of Son of Heaven when he became an emperor at the age of 13. The Qin dynasty unified China and began to build a great wall across the nation to protect it from northern invaders. This wall is known as the Great Wall of China.

The Han dynasty ruled China from 206 B.C. to A.D. 220. During the Han dynasty, paper was first made, and the Silk Road became a major trade route. The Silk Road spanned 4,350 miles (7,000.6 km) from eastern China west to the Mediterranean Sea. It was the main trade route between China and Europe for more than 1,000 years. The Silk Road was named for the fine cloth made from a process that the Chinese kept secret for centuries. Chinese merchants traded silk

A portrait of Mao Zedong hangs over the main gate at Tiananmen Square, in the heart of Beijing. Mao rebuilt the square as a site for public displays, ceremonies, parades, and celebrations.

for European glass and perfume. They traveled the Silk Road in caravans and used camels to carry their goods. The Tang dynasty ruled China from A.D. 618 to 907. This period is called the Golden Age of Chinese history, because education, art, and literature thrived under the Tang rulers.

The last dynasty, called Qing, ended in 1912. When it fell, the Nationalist Party took over and established the Republic of China. The Nationalist Party was founded by Sun Yat-sen. He wanted China to become a modern republic. People who did not want China to be a republic organized the Chinese Communist Party. When the Communists defeated the Nationalists in 1949, Mao Zedong became China's leader and changed the country's name to the People's Republic of China. Under communism, Mao took control of China's land, farms, and industries. Many people lived together in communes and shared food and work duties. Foreigners were not allowed in China, and the Chinese could not leave the country. Mao started the Cultural Revolution, which was responsible for the destruction of priceless artworks and even buildings, such as temples. Deng Xiaoping took over as the leader of the Communist Party when Mao died in 1976. He opened China to foreign travelers. He improved the Chinese economy by modernizing farming, industry, defense, and science. This book will teach you more about China and how to draw some of its sights and symbols. You start with one shape and add other shapes to the drawing. New steps are shown in red. Directions are under each step. Before you start, gather the following supplies to draw China's sights and symbols:

- A sketch pad
- An eraser
- A number 2 pencil
- A pencil sharpener

These are some of the shapes and drawing terms you need to know to draw China's sights and symbols:

— Horizontal line

◯ Oval

▭ Rectangle

▰ Shading

〜 Squiggle

▱ Trapezoid

△ Triangle

| Vertical line

〜 Wavy line

More About China

China is the third-largest country in the world. Only Russia and Canada are larger. China has about 3.7 million square miles (9.6 million sq km) of land and occupies almost one-fourth of Asia. China borders 14 countries and 3 large bodies of water, which are the Yellow Sea, the East China Sea, and the South China Sea.

Beijing, located in northeastern China, is the country's capital. It is the second-most-populated city, with 8,450,000 people. Beijing began as a trading post 3,000 years ago. The most-populated city in China is Shanghai with 11,800,000 people. Hong Kong was a British colony from 1842 to 1997. Today Hong Kong is one of the world's busiest shipping centers. Of China's many islands, Taiwan is the most important. It belongs to China but has a separate, democratic government.

China has the largest population in the world with about 1.3 billion people. The Han Chinese are descendants of the Han dynasty and make up 92 percent of the population. There are 50 minority

The Tibetan plateau, along southwestern China, is so high that, at more than 13,123 feet (4,000 m), it is called the Roof of the World. A plateau is a broad, high, flat piece of land. The Tibetan plateau is bordered by the Himalayas, the highest mountains on Earth.

groups that make up the rest of the population. The Zhuangs from southwest China are the largest minority. Mongols of northern China are a minority that ruled China from 1279 to 1368. The Tibetans are a small minority who live near the Himalayan Mountains in southwest China. The tallest of these mountains is Mount Everest, which is nearly 5.5 miles (8.9 km) high at 29,028 feet (8,847.7 m). Mount Everest borders China and Nepal.

Different dialects of the Chinese language are spoken in different areas of the country. However, the Mandarin dialect is the common language of China. More people speak Chinese than any other language in the world. China is an agricultural country that produces more food than any other country in the world. China's main crops include rice, wheat, tea, and soybeans. Other agricultural products include cotton, silk, sheep, and goats. China has many natural resources, including coal, iron ore, and zinc. The country's top industries are rolled steel, electronics, garments, cement, oil, and textiles.

Victoria Peak is Hong Kong Island's highest peak at 1,810 feet (552 m) above sea level and one of the island's most visited sites. This is a view of Hong Kong from Peak Victoria.

The Artist Ma Yuan

Landscape painting is one of the most prized forms of Chinese art, because it shows the Earth's majesty and man's relationship to his surroundings. Landscapes are pictures or drawings of natural scenery. Landscape painting reached its peak during the southern Song dynasty, which lasted from A.D. 1127 to 1280. Artists from the southern Song dynasty loved nature and wanted to celebrate its beauty. The artists painted simple scenes of mountains and water, often leaving sections of their paintings empty.

One of the greatest masters of landscape painting during the southern Song dynasty was Ma Yuan. Born in 1190, Ma Yuan is called One-Corner Ma, because he liked to paint a scene in one corner of the canvas and leave the rest empty. Instead of painting a scene in great detail, Ma focused on capturing the spirit and beauty of nature. An example of Ma's one-corner paintings is *Watching the Deer by a Pine Shaded Stream*. In this painting, Ma used black ink on a silk canvas. He chose a silk canvas because silk absorbs the ink. When color is absorbed, it quickly spreads and fades into lighter shades. Ma also used ink washes, which are thin layers of ink and water, to make objects fade even more. In this painting, Ma used the washes to make the background appear cloudy or misty. This gave the painting a peaceful, almost mystical quality. The water, trees, and deer represent a celebration of nature. The person lying down and watching the deer represents man's humble place in nature. Delicate branches of pine trees stretch across the landscape to complete this scene of southern China.

During the southern Song Dynasty, Ma Yuan created *Watching the Deer by a Pine Shaded Stream*. It was done in ink and light color on silk and measures 11.33" x 10.23" (24.8 cm x 26 cm). Although there are people in the landscape, the stream, the rocks, and the pine trees take center stage.

Map of China

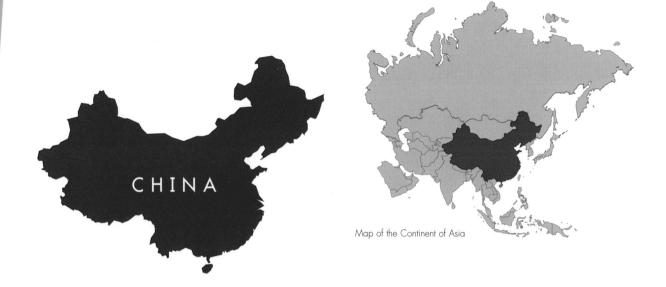

CHINA

Map of the Continent of Asia

Because of China's size, its geography is diverse. The Plateau of Tibet is in southwest China. In the northwest is Taklimakan, China's largest desert. The Mongolian grasslands, the Gobi Desert, and the Manchurian Plain are in northern China. China's northeast is made up of hills, plains, and river valleys. This area is an important agricultural center. The 3,915-mile (6,300-km) Yangtze River is the longest river in Asia and is one of Asia's most important trade routes. The Yellow River is called the Cradle of Chinese Civilization, because people lived by the river more than 4,000 years ago. The Grand Canal, which covers 1,105 miles (1,800 km), was built in the fifth century B.C., to move armies during times of war.

1

Draw a rectangle. This is a guide shape, so draw lightly. You will erase this shape later.

2

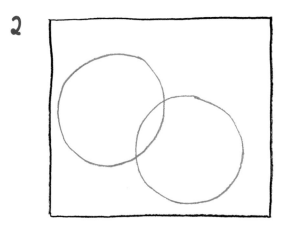

Draw two circles that overlap each other. Notice their placement inside the square.

3

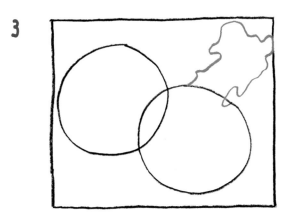

On top of the right circle, draw the shape shown in red. Before you draw, check out the map of China on the opposite page.

4

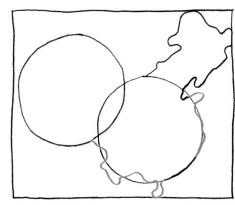

Using wavy lines, outline the edge of the right circle to draw the eastern border of China. Notice that some areas stick out of the circle.

5

Use the left circle to shape western China.

6

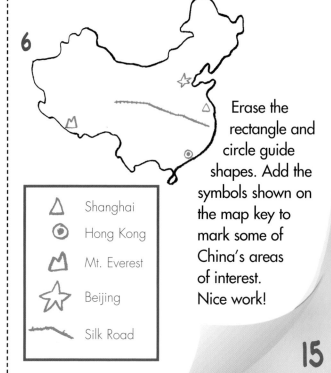

△	Shanghai
◉	Hong Kong
⋈	Mt. Everest
☆	Beijing
～	Silk Road

Erase the rectangle and circle guide shapes. Add the symbols shown on the map key to mark some of China's areas of interest. Nice work!

Flag of China

China's flag was designed by Zeng Liansong. The flag was adopted in 1949. Zeng Liansong was an amateur artist from Shanghai. An amateur is someone who does something as a hobby or for free. Zeng thought that the flag should reflect the power of the Communist state and the culture of the country.

The red background of China's flag stands for the Communist Party. Red is also a favorite color of the Chinese. The Chinese consider red to be a color of good luck. In the top left corner of the flag is a large yellow star. Four smaller yellow stars form a half circle around the big star. Yellow represents the Sun and light. The four stars symbolize the four social classes defined by Mao Zedong. These classes included workers, peasants, merchants, and aristocrats.

1

Draw a rectangle.

2

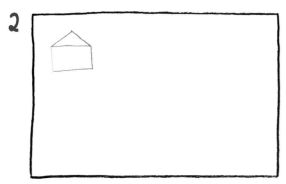

Lightly draw a small house by stacking a triangle on top of a rectangle. This shape will help you to draw the five-pointed star.

3

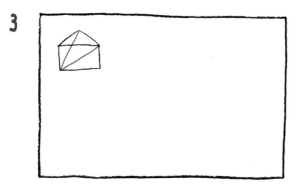

Draw a V shape inside the house. Make sure the points of the V shape touch the correct corners of the house, just like in the picture.

4

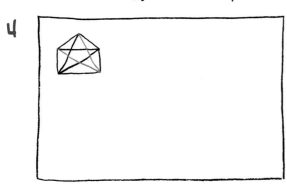

Draw another *V* shape as shown in red.

5

Erase the house. Your five-pointed star should look like the one above.

6

Carefully erase the lines inside the star. Use steps 2 through 6 to help you draw the four smaller stars. Notice that the stars are arranged on a curve.

7

Shade the background, and you are done.

17

The Giant Panda

Many Chinese regard the giant panda as China's national animal, although it hasn't officially been adopted as a national symbol. The giant panda is black and white. Pandas live in China's mountains and bamboo forests. An adult panda is from 4 to 6 feet (1.2–1.8 m) tall and weighs about 220 pounds (99.8 kg). Giant pandas are herbivores, which means that they eat only plants. The giant panda eats mostly bamboo shoots, which are giant grasses with hard stalks. The panda has a special front toe that is used like a thumb to grab the bamboo from the ground. With its claws and teeth, the panda then strips the hard bamboo stalk to get to the softer stalk inside. China gave two giant pandas named Tian Tian and Mei Xiang to the United States as a gift of friendship. You can see them at the National Zoo in Washington, D.C.

1 Begin with the outline of the tree trunk. Draw two slanted lines next to each other. Notice that the lines slant toward the left.

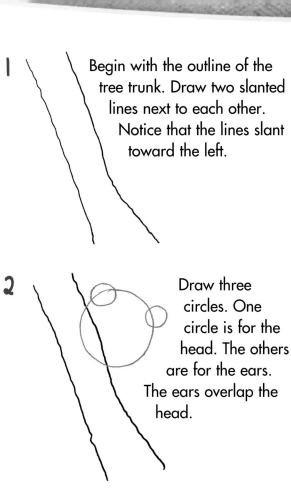

2 Draw three circles. One circle is for the head. The others are for the ears. The ears overlap the head.

3 Add two oval shapes. Notice the placement of the shapes before you draw them.

4 Add another oval. This oval overlaps the left oval that you drew in the previous step.

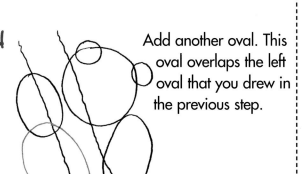

5 Using the ovals that you drew in step 3 as guides, shape the two arms of the giant panda bear.

6 Erase extra lines, and smooth out the curves of the panda's body. Add pointy claws to the arms that you drew in the previous step.

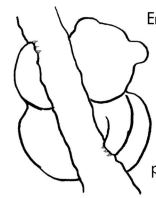

7 Draw the giant panda's face. First draw the roundish nose. Next draw the eyes.

8 Add the nose. Shade your panda and the tree trunk. Notice where the shading is dark and where it is light.

The Tree Peony

   The peony has been the favorite flower of the Chinese people for 1,500 years. It became China's royal flower during the Qing dynasty. However, the tree peony hasn't been officially adopted as China's national flower. The tree peony was nicknamed the King of Flowers during the Tang dynasty. The tree peony is actually a shrub. A shrub is a bush that has several stems that branch out close to the ground. The tree peony can grow to be from 4 to 6 feet (1.2–1.8 m) high with large flowers that range from 6 to 12 inches (15.2–30.5 cm) across. Peony blossoms bloom in many colors, including pink, red, white, and purple. Luoyang, located east of Xi'an near the Yellow River, is famous for growing peonies. The city even hosts a peony ceremony every April 20 to honor China's favorite flower!

1 Draw a tiny circle inside a large circle.

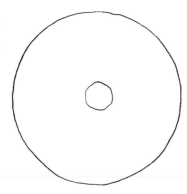

2 Begin to add the petals. Each petal has a different shape. They are all made using soft, curved lines.

3 Keep adding petals. Some are thin because they are turned sideways. The petals don't have to look perfect so have fun drawing them!

4 Fill in the larger petals toward the outer circle. The more petals you draw, the fuller your peony will look.

5 As you add more petals, notice the way the edges get wavier.

6 Let the last petals spill a little over the edge of the large circle.

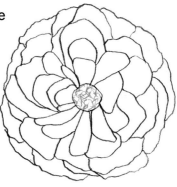

7 Carefully erase the circle guide shape. Draw squiggly lines inside the center of the flower.

8 Shade the petals. Don't shade the entire flower! Lightly shade between only some of the petals.

The Red-Crowned Crane

The red-crowned crane is considered the national bird of China. The Chinese believe that this bird is a sign of good luck and long life. There are fewer than 2,000 red-crowned cranes in the world, and half of them live in China. The bird gets its name from the patch of red skin on top of its head. At 5 feet (1.5 m) tall, the red-crowned crane is one of the world's largest birds. It weighs about 20 pounds (9 kg) and has a wingspan of up to 8 feet (2.4 m). Its body is white with black markings on its neck and wings. The red-crowned crane prefers to live near freshwater marshes, crop fields, and rice fields, where food is plentiful. It uses its sharp, pointed beak to spear insects, fish, rodents, and grasses. To communicate with each other, red-crowned cranes perform a special dance that consists of head bobs, jumps, and bows.

1

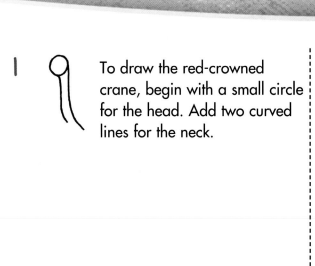

To draw the red-crowned crane, begin with a small circle for the head. Add two curved lines for the neck.

4

Draw the tail. Notice the ends of the tail are shaggy. The tail comes down to the middle of its hind leg.

2

For the body, draw a teardrop. Add a triangle for a beak.

5

Erase extra lines. Your crane should look like the drawing on this step. Add a dark dot for an eye.

3

Draw two long, thin legs. Add triangular feet. Make sure the knees and tops of the legs are rounded. Look at the photo on the opposite page for help.

6

Shade your crane, and you are done. Nice work.

23

Peking Man

In 1929, archaeologists uncovered caves in Zhoukoudian, a village 30 miles (48.3 km) from Beijing. They found the teeth and bones of a species of people who lived 500,000 to 300,000 years ago! They named this species *Homo erectus pekinensis* or Peking Man. This species may have lived in the Zhoukoudian caves for about 250 million years. Archaeologists believe that Peking Man had the facial features of an ape but could walk upright like a human. From fossils found at the site, archaeologists learned that Peking Man made fires to keep warm and to cook food. Stone tools and bones of tigers and bears were also found. Peking Man hunted these animals for food.

1  Begin by drawing an oval for the head. Add a curved, vertical line for the front part of the body. Next draw a horizontal line for the arm.

2  Draw the stick using two vertical lines that close at the top. Add an oval shape above the head. This will be the outline of the hand holding a rock.

3 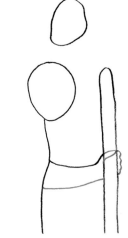 Draw the left arm. His hands are gripping the stick. First draw a horizontal line beneath the line you drew in step 1. Next draw his hand.

4 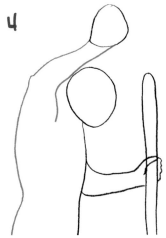 Add a long, bending line for the raised arm and the back. Next add another bent line near the head.

5  Add wavy and curved lines to the raised hand. It should look as if the hand is holding a rock.

6 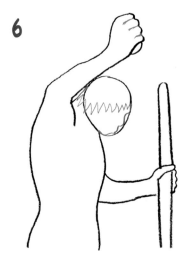 Add detail to the fingers. Draw a zigzag line for the hair. Shape the face using the oval guide shape you drew in step 1. Can you see the outline of the forehead, eyes, nose, and chin? Erase extra lines.

7 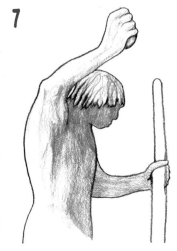 Shade your drawing, and you are done!

Confucius

Confucius (551–479 B.C.) was China's greatest philosopher and teacher. He developed a philosophy called Confucianism that has impacted China for more than 2,000 years. Confucianism stresses the importance of people achieving peace and harmony in their lives. He believed that order and moral standards were necessary for a country to exist. He taught that order is kept by following Chinese customs, practicing good manners, and showing respect for others. After Confucius died, a temple was built in his honor in Qufu, located southeast of Beijing. The huge temple complex is made of more than 400 buildings, including Confucius's library, the hall where he taught students, and his living quarters.

1

Begin the temple by drawing a rectangle.

2

Add a horizontal line.

3

Draw the second level by adding a long shape that curls up at the corners. Add another long shape on top.

4

Draw a roof that widens at the top. To do this, draw two slanted vertical lines and then connect the lines with a horizontal line. Draw a small rectangle in the center of the second level. Add a door on the first level.

5

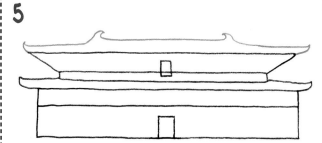

Add the top part of the roof. Notice that it looks like the shape you drew in step 3. Make sure the ends curl up at the corners. Also draw the two hooked shapes on top of the roof.

6

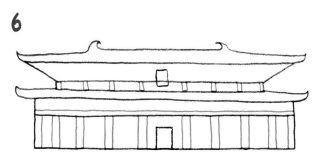

Draw vertical lines for the two rows of columns. Draw a horizontal line above the columns on the first floor.

7

Shade your drawing. Notice that the darkest areas are under the sections that curl. The shading should also be dark between the columns.

The Caves of the Thousand Buddhas

The Caves of the Thousand Buddhas are located on the Silk Road near Dunhuang in northwest China. These caves house some of the world's best examples of Buddhist art. Buddhist monks who traveled along the Silk Road introduced Buddhism to China. In A.D. 366, a monk carved the first cave out of a rocky cliff. During the next 1,000 years, more caves were carved into the hillside. Inside the 492 caves that remain there today, there are 2,415 painted sculptures and nearly 484,376 square feet (45,000 sq m) of paintings on the walls and ceilings. The paintings include pictures of Buddha, landscapes, animals, heavenly creatures, and military parades.

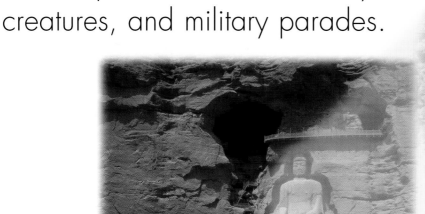

1  Draw a rectangle with rounded corners. This is the head.

5  Erase extra lines. Draw vertical lines to Buddha's shoulders. Notice that these lines curve at the bottom.

2 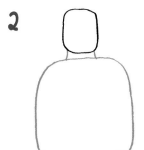 Draw a bigger square with rounded corners. Connect it to the head with two small lines.

6  Add a curved line on top of the Buddha's head. Add a curved rectangle shape on top of the head. Draw curved lines for eyebrows and eyes.

3  Add a rounded square for the lower half of the Buddha. His legs are covered by a robe.

7  Add a line for the nose, and draw the mouth.

4 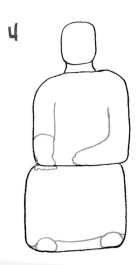 Use curved lines to draw the arms. Notice that the carved rock has been worn with age, so the arms are simple and rounded. Add two round shapes for feet and a horizontal line for the bottom of the robe.

8  Shade your Buddha. Pay close attention to the shadows around the face.

The Great Wall of China

In 770 B.C., feudal landowners needed to protect their land from northern invaders. They began to build high walls around their property. These walls were joined to form the base of the Great Wall during the Qin dynasty. The wall was extended and rebuilt during the Ming dynasty, 600 years ago. The Great Wall runs from Jiayu Pass in western China and stretches eastward to the Yellow Sea. The Great Wall is more than 4,000 miles (6,437.4 km) long, which is more than 1,000 miles (1,609.3 km) longer than the distance between New York City and San Francisco! The walls are 15 to 30 feet (4.6 to 9.1 m) thick and about 25 feet (7.6 m) high. The walls are made of tree branches, stone, sand, clay, and other materials. One historian claimed that the amount of materials used to build the wall would be enough to circle Earth five times!

1 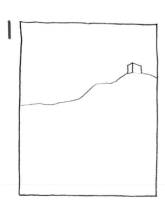 Draw a rectangle. Add a wavy line that turns into a hill. On top of the hill, draw a 3-D box.

2 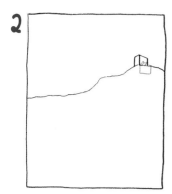 Draw small lines inside the 3-D box. Add the first section of the wall. To do this, you will need to draw another box underneath the box you drew in the last step.

3 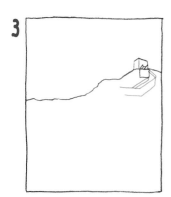 Add diagonal lines to show the wall winding down the hill. A diagonal line is a line drawn at a slant.

4 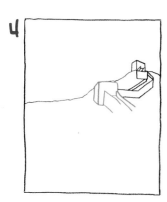 Draw another 3-D box. These boxes are stations for the soldiers who guarded the wall. Add more diagonal lines that slope down from the new station you just drew.

5 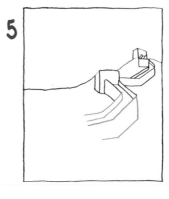 Draw more diagonal lines that turn to the left. The space between the lines should be greater than the space between the lines you drew in earlier steps.

6 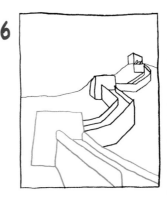 Draw the final station and the walls. Good work! On a flat surface, you were able to draw the Great Wall so that it appears to be seen at a distance. This is an art term called perspective.

7 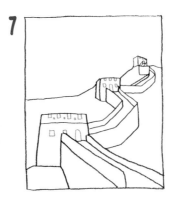 Add windows and arched doorways. Draw small squares along the top of each station. Soldiers hid behind the taller parts of the wall when they were fighting the enemy.

8  Erase extra lines. Draw small rectangles to show bricklike details on the Great Wall. Shade your drawing.

The Terra-Cotta Warriors

In 1974, farmers who were digging a well near Xi'an discovered a treasure of ancient China. They found Qin Shi Huang's mausoleum, filled with an army of soldiers sculpted of terra-cotta. According to historians, it took 700,000 workers 36 years to build the mausoleum and to make the terra-cotta warriors to guard Qin's tomb when he died in 210 B.C. So far, about 7,000 life-size soldiers have been unearthed along with terra-cotta horses, wooden chariots, and real weapons. In the main chamber, the warriors are placed in 11 columns of 4 or 5 side by side. Each sculpted warrior has a different expression on his face! The uniform he wears identifies his position in the army. For example, a foot soldier wears a long tunic, or a sleeveless top, over his regular shirt and short pants.

1 Begin with an oval head. Add a round collar.

2 Add the basic shape of his upper body, or torso. It is made with a rounded rectangle that is narrower at the bottom.

3 Add the rough outline of two arms.

4 Add the curved shape of the hairline. Draw an upside-down *U* shape on top of his head.

5 Draw diagonal lines on each shoulder. This is part of the soldier's armor. Add a vertical line at his hip.

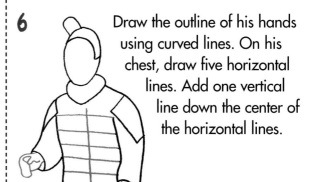

6 Draw the outline of his hands using curved lines. On his chest, draw five horizontal lines. Add one vertical line down the center of the horizontal lines.

7 Add two curved eyebrows, two almond-shaped eyes and the nose. Add an ear and a mustache that bends down. Add a small, triangular beard.

8 Shade your drawing. Add details to the armor, such as small buttons.

33

Kung Fu and the Shaolin Monastery

In the sixth century A.D., an Indian Buddhist priest named Tamo arrived in China. He stopped at a Buddhist monastery called Shaolin. Tamo noticed that the monks were not strong enough to perform Buddhist meditation exercises, so he taught the monks some exercises to build strength. Eventually, these exercises developed into martial arts, which are different styles of self-defense. One of these styles is called kung fu. Kung fu is based on self defense and how to avoid conflict. Kung fu teaches a person to be responsible for his or her actions and to respect others. People who practice kung fu do not attack first. They simply defend themselves from the attacks of others by stopping the attacks with special kicks or hand movements. Many of the movements are named for animals that they imitate, such as the dragon, the tiger, or the monkey.

1 Begin by drawing an oval for the head. Add a slanted rectangle. Connect the two shapes with small lines for the neck.

2 Add the basic outline of the arms and hands. Start with the left side and then draw the right side. Before you start, carefully look at the red shapes.

3 Using curved and straight lines, sketch the outline of the legs. Notice the monk's interesting position. One leg is tucked under his hips, and one leg bends out to the side.

4 Next draw the details of the arms and hands. Use curved lines because the arms are muscular. Notice how the monk is holding one hand so that the palm faces us. The other palm points to the ground. Add a V shape at the neck for the collar of the monk's top.

5 Using curved lines, add the rounded edges of the monk's shirt, pants, and shoes. Follow the straight lines of your sketch.

6 Start drawing the face. Draw the monk's eyebrows, nose, and ears.

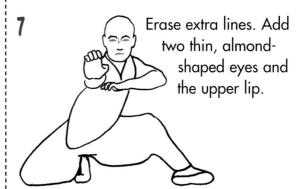

7 Erase extra lines. Add two thin, almond-shaped eyes and the upper lip.

8 Shade your drawing, and you're done.

The Forbidden City

Located in the center of Beijing is the Forbidden City, the largest palace complex in the world. According to legend, there are 9,999 rooms. It sits on almost 78 acres (32 ha) of land. The palace complex was built in the fifteenth century and was the home of the Ming and Qing emperors until 1924. The complex was called the Forbidden City because no one could enter without permission from the emperor. The Forbidden City is surrounded by 35-foot-high (11-m-high) walls. It contains royal palaces, courtyards, halls, government buildings, and an area for special prayer ceremonies, called the Temple of Heaven. The most beautiful building in the Temple of Heaven is the Hall of Prayer for Good Harvest.

1

Draw a long, thin rectangle. Add a slanted rectangle on top.

2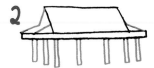

Add small diagonal lines on both sides of the slanted rectangle. On the left side, add a bent line from the top of the slanted rectangle to the top corner of the long, thin rectangle. Add seven columns. Columns are posts that support a building.

3

Curl the ends of the long, thin rectangle so that they sweep upward. Next add lines between the columns to create the lower part of the building. Draw three more columns under the center of the building. Add another section of the building on the right. Curl its roof corner as you did on the main building.

4

Erase extra lines. Add two curving shapes to the corners of the roof. Add arches between the columns. Use straight lines to make two more buildings.

5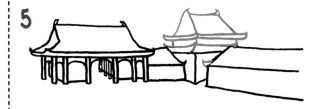

Using vertical, diagonal, and horizontal lines, add the upper stories to the center building. Work from bottom to top. Curl the corners of the roof sections.

6

Add windows. Erase any extra lines that you don't need. Draw a triangle in the top section of the tallest building.

7

Shade the buildings. Make the windows dark. Good work!

Chinese New Year

Chinese New Year falls in January or February and lasts for 15 days. It is the most important holiday for Chinese people throughout the world. Chinese New Year is a time to do things that will bring good luck in the coming year. To prepare for New Year, the Chinese clean their homes, buy new clothes, pay all debts, and stock up on food for family dinners. Many Chinese put up red decorations and give their children red envelopes stuffed with money for good luck. On the last day of Chinese New Year, the holiday ends with a dragon parade. The dragon is made of brightly colored silk cloth and paper. It is attached to bamboo poles. Boys hold on to the poles

and dance along the street, which makes the dragon look as if it is moving through the air. The dragon stands for power, luck, and success.

1 Begin by drawing the egg shape of the dragon's head. Add a teardrop shape to the top right of the egg shape for the dragon's eye.

2 Add the snakelike neck and body. For the neck, draw two lines that come down from the narrow part of the egg shape. For the body, draw a curved round shape. Notice that it looks kind of like a doughnut!

3 Begin at the top with the lines that make up the nose. Then add a curvy shape for the inside of the mouth. It looks like a bubble-letter V shape on its side. Finally add the round chin and the curve of the jaw.

4 Add shaggy lines to the chin. Draw pointy teeth inside the bubble using V shapes as shown.

5 Add a curved line for the bottom lip. Add curved lines to the jaw. Draw tiny triangles on the jaw. Then work on the eye. Add curls like fire above the almond-shaped eye. Draw a dark eyeball.

6 Add spikes to the jaw. Then add spikes to the dragon's back.

7 Draw repeated U shapes to create the pattern of the dragon's scales. This will take time, but be patient. The scales are an important part of the dragon's body.

8 Erase extra lines. Add detail, and shade your scary and powerful dragon.

Tiananmen Square

Mao Zedong rebuilt Tiananmen Square in the 1950s. The square is the largest public square in the world. It covers about 100 acres (40.5 ha) and can hold one million people! Thousands of students demonstrated in Tiananmen Square in 1989 for government reforms and political freedom. They built a 33-foot (10-m) statue that resembled the Statue of Liberty and named it the Goddess of Democracy. The government ordered the army to stop the demonstration. Soldiers destroyed the Goddess of Democracy and wounded and even killed students who refused to leave the square. The demonstration turned into a tragedy. However, it did lead to changes. People now have the freedom to own businesses. Some villages even hold elections for local leaders! This is an important political right for people to hold.

1 Although the Goddess of Democracy was destroyed, you can still draw the statue based on the photograph shown on the opposite page. Draw an oval head and a short vertical line for the neck. Next draw a long *T* shape. Notice that the tail of the *T* shape is slightly curved.

2 Add a horizontal line for the shoulders. Draw two raised, bent arms using diagonal lines.

3 Add a small line to form the neck. Draw the left arm using curved lines. At the end of the arm, draw the hand to show that it is wrapped around the torch.

4 Add another arm and hand reaching up to hold the torch. Draw the body of the figure using a long rectangle shape that gets wider at the bottom. The Goddess of Democracy is wearing a dress, so you won't draw her legs or feet. Erase extra lines.

5 Add a zigzag line that curves around her head. This is her hair. Give the figure a base to stand on by adding two horizontal lines, one on each side of the bottom of her robe.

6 Draw a square for the handle of the torch. Draw a bowl shape on top of it. Next draw the flame on top.

7 Draw a curved line on each arm to show the sleeves. Add an ear. Draw curved eyebrows. Next draw the eyes. Add a curved line for the nose and straight lines for the mouth.

8  Shade your drawing. Doesn't the Goddess of Democracy resemble the Statue of Liberty in New York City?

Shanghai

Shanghai means "on the sea" in Chinese. Shanghai is known for its harbor, which is one of the largest in the world. With access to the Pacific Ocean, the city has served as an international trade center for more than a century. The city's location is one reason the government has spent 40 billion dollars to rebuild it. The government wants Shanghai to become a symbol of modern China and a world-class financial and trade center. More than 1,000 skyscrapers have been built since 1990, including the Oriental Pearl Tower, pictured here. These buildings, combined with new industrial sites, shopping malls, hotels, and a stock exchange, are quickly making Shanghai one of the leading business centers of the twenty-first century.

1  Draw two lines for your guides. Draw a long vertical line and a short horizontal line toward the bottom.

5  Draw two long vertical lines to the left and right of the last step. At the top draw two curved lines. Next draw twelve vertical lines paired in twos between each horizontal pair.

2 Draw two circles. The circle on top is slightly smaller than the one below it. Notice the placement of the two circles.

6 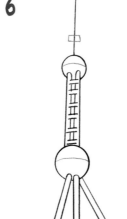 Add a rectangle at the top of the tower. Then add two curved lines inside each circle. Erase your guides.

3 Draw five lines under the lower circle. Notice that the left and middle lines are connected with a curved line on top.

7  Shade your drawing and then you're done.

4  Draw twelve horizontal lines at a slight angle. Notice how they are paired in twos.

Timeline

1600–1100 B.C.	Shang dynasty.
551–479 B.C.	Life of Confucius.
221 B.C.	Qin Shi Huang becomes emperor, unites China, and begins building the Great Wall.
221–206 B.C.	Qin dynasty.
206 B.C.–A.D. 220	Han dynasty. Paper is made for the first time in history.
A.D. 618–907	The Tang dynasty rules during China's Golden Age.
1279	The Mongols conquer China and make Beijing the capital.
1368–1644	Ming dynasty.
1644–1912	Qing dynasty.
1839–1842	The first Opium War with Great Britain occurs.
1856–1860	The second Opium War with Great Britain occurs.
1911	The Nationalist Party is founded by Sun Yat-sen.
	Sun Yat-sen establishes the Republic of China.
1921	The Communist Party is founded by Mao Zedong.
1949	The Communists defeat the Nationalists.
	China becomes a Communist State.
	Mao Zedong calls the nation the People's Republic of China.
1966	The Cultural Revolution begins.
1972	Richard Nixon is the first U.S. president to visit China.
1976	Mao Zedong dies.
1978	Deng Xiaoping becomes the leader of the People's Republic.
1989	The Tiananmen Square demonstrations occur.

China Fact List

Official Name	People's Republic of China
Area	3,696,100 square miles (9,572,900 sq km)
Population	1,274,915,000 people
Capital	Beijing, population 8,450,000
Most-Populated City	Shanghai, population 11,800,000
Industries	Rolled steel, cement, oil, textiles
Agriculture	Rice, wheat, soybeans, tea, silk, cotton, sheep, goats
Natural Resources	Coal, iron ore, zinc
Favorite Flower	Tree peony
Favorite Bird	Red-crowned crane
Favorite Animal	Giant panda
Highest Mountain Peak	Mount Everest, 29,028 feet (8.847.7 m)
Longest River	Yangtze River, 3,915 miles (6,300.6 km)
National Language	Mandarin Chinese
Major Festivals	Chinese New Year, Dragon Boat Festival
National Drink	Tea

Glossary

access (AK-ses) A way to get somewhere easily.

archaeologists (ar-kee-AH-luh-jists) People who study the remains of peoples to understand how they lived.

aristocrats (uh-RIS-tuh-krats) Members of the wealthy upper class.

Buddhist (BOO-dist) Having to do with the faith of Buddhism.

canvas (KAN-ves) A cloth surface that is used for a painting.

caravans (KAR-uh-vanz) Groups of travelers who carry their supplies and travel in lines.

ceremony (SER-ih-moh-nee) A series of actions done on certain occasions.

chariots (CHAR-ee-uts) Two-wheeled battle cars pulled by horses.

communes (KAH-myoonz) Groups of people who live together.

communism (KOM-yuh-nih-zem) When the government owns property and goods that are to be shared equally by all the people.

complex (KOM-pleks) A large group of buildings.

conflict (KON-flikt) A fight or a struggle.

culture (KUL-chur) The beliefs, practices, and arts of a group of people.

customs (KUS-tumz) Practices common to many in an area or a social class.

defeated (dih-FEET-ed) To have won against someone in a contest or battle.

delicate (DEH-lih-kit) Easily broken or harmed.

democratic (deh-muh-KRA-tik) In favor of democracy, a system in which people choose their leaders.

demonstration (deh-mun-STRAY-shun) Public gatherings for a person or a cause.

descendants (dih-SEN-dents) People born of a certain family or group.

dialects (DY-uh-lekts) Different ways that a language is spoken in different regions or places.

diverse (dy-VERS) Different.

dynasty (DY-nas-tee) A series of rulers who belong to the same family.

emperor (EM-per-er) The ruler of an empire, or several countries.

feudal (FYOO-dul) Having to do with an ancient system in which people worked and fought for a landowner who protected them.

historian (hih-STOR-ee-un) Someone who studies the past.

imitate (IH-muh-tayt) To copy something or someone.

impacted (im-PAKT-ed) Had an effect on someone or something.

industries (IN-dus-treez) Moneymaking businesses in which many people work and make money producing particular products.

invaders (in-VAYD-erz) People who enter a place to attack and conquer it.

mausoleum (mah-suh-LEE-um) A grave that is above ground.

minority (my-NOR-ih-tee) Having to do with a group of people that is in some way different from the larger part of a population.

monastery (MAH-nuh-ster-ee) A house where people who have taken vows of faith live and work.

philosopher (fih-LAH-suh-fer) A person who tries to discover and to understand the basic nature of knowledge.

process (PRAH-ses) The series of steps for making or doing something.

reforms (rih-FORMZ) Changes or improvements.

republic (ree-PUB-lik) A form of government in which the authority belongs to the people.

resources (REE-sors-ez) Supplies or sources of energy or useful materials.

revolution (reh-vuh-LOO-shun) A complete change in something, such as a government.

sculptures (SKULP-cherz) Figures that are carved or formed out of stone or other materials.

species (SPEE-sheez) A single kind of plant or animal. All people are one species.

stalks (STOKS) Slender parts of plants that support the rest of the plants.

symbols (SIM-bulz) Objects or designs that stand for something else.

terra-cotta (ter-uh-KAH-tuh) A type of brownish orange clay.

thrived (THRYVD) Grew strong.

tragedy (TRA-jeh-dee) A very sad event.

Index

Web Sites

Due to the changing nature of Internet links, PowerKids Press has developed an online list of Web sites related to the subject of this book. This site is updated regularly. Please use this link to access the list:
www.powerkidslinks.com/kgdc/china/